THE STORY I TELL

REBECCA WHITED

Higher
Ground
Books &
Media
HGBM

Scripture taken from the HOLY BIBLE, NEW INTERNATIONAL
VERSION®. NIV®. Copyright © 1973, 1978, 1984 by International Bible
Society. Used by permission of Zondervan. All rights reserved worldwide.

Higher Ground Books & Media
P.O. Box 2914
Springfield, OH 45501-2914
www.highergroundbooksandmedia.com
1-937-970-0554

Because of the dynamic nature of the Internet, any web addresses or links
contained in this book may have changed since publication and may no
longer be valid. The views expressed in the work are solely those of the
author and do not necessarily reflect the views of the publisher, and the
publisher hereby disclaims any responsibility for them.

Any people depicted in stock imagery are being used for illustrative
purposes only.

ISBN (Paperback): 978-1-955368-33-9

Printed in the United States of America 2023

THE STORY
I TELL

REBECCA WHITED

We all have a story to tell. We have a past. We are in the present. We have a future. A lot of our stories revolve around how Jesus came into our lives and changed the direction of our path. Healed us of our past, then filled our future with hope and possibilities. We often refer to the story we tell as our testimony. We are all called to share our testimony with others. In Mark 5:19, Jesus tells the man He just healed of demon possession to "Go home to your own people and tell them how much the Lord has done for you and how He has had mercy on you". It also says that he did just that and all the people were amazed. Our very own testimonies are powerful tools for God. He uses them to heal others that are hurting or struggling in the same manner that we are. A unique concept about sharing your testimony with other people is that your testimony is not up for discussion. When you say "I felt afraid" nobody can debate how you felt. When you say I felt like "the weight of the world had been lifted off my shoulders", nobody can debate that. Unlike discussing scripture where some might be in the habit of disagreeing with others, with your testimony they cannot deny how you felt and what happened to you.

Testimonies are also never ceasing. Though often thought of as how you came to know Jesus, you should have not one testimony, but many. When we set our eyes on Jesus, we can see how He shapes our lives on a daily basis. We can see His thumb print on our circumstances and situations, even struggles, if not more so. As we look back on our life, it is those stories, AKA testimonies that Peter speaks of in 1 Peter 3. In verse 15 he says, "But in your hearts revere Christ as Lord. Always be prepared to give an answer to everyone who asks you to give the reason for the hope that you have". This particular section in 1 Peter, he is talking about persecution, but I think it still stands, even without persecution. As believers, we should always be prepared to give an account.

We have our first testimony which often can be the most powerful because it shows how God took us from sinful broken worldly people and had mercy on us. It gives hope to other people that they too can be restored. The testimonies that follow are how God has moved us from point A to point B to point C and so on. If we continue to seek Him and grow in our faith, we will always have a continuous supply of testimonies.

It is important to share these testimonies because we are not alone in this walk, and our circumstances are not that rare or exclusive that others cannot relate or cannot begin to understand. Those thoughts of doubt are lies that come from Satan in an attempt to bind us in our mind. It's that vulnerability that comes from sharing our testimony with others, be it on a public or more intimate level, that God can use to tear down walls and open hearts.

In Bits and Pieces, my first book that God called me to write, it is that vulnerability that I shared. This time around will be slightly different. The following testimonies are biblical fiction. What I mean by that is, the facts of their life are taken from scripture, but I took liberty to add human feelings and emotions to describe how they might have presented their testimony. To demonstrate that even the most obscure people in scripture would have still had a testimony to share. Just as you do too. At the end of each testimony, I will include the scriptures that I used to gather information about their lives. After reading these testimonies it is my hope that you will feel encouraged to share your own testimony(ies), whether it is at a revival, church service, social media, or one-on-one. God will use us AND our testimony if we get out of our own way. This is The Story I Tell.

MUST READ

The following testimonies are the compilation of characters of scripture and my imagination of how they may have felt and lived. The characters are rooted in Biblical truth, but please remember that I have filled in their back stories and emotions with my imagination. At the end of each chapter are the scripture sections that I used to build the basis for the character. Please read those scriptures for yourself and learn what is and is not the imagination. It is my hope that these characters will intrigue you to dig into scripture and meet them for yourselves, as well as encourage you to share your own testimony.

CONTENTS

Jochebed

My name is Jochebed. I know you are probably wondering who in the world is Jochebed. Most of you know me as Moses' mother. Maybe some of you can relate. Perhaps you are known as Joseph's mom or Cornelius' mom, but do not forget that you too have a name. You too have a testimony, beyond the identity of Mother. And while my story is also the story of Moses' birth, it is the story of God's love and His amazing blessing that He gives us when we are obedient. That, my friend, is what I want you to know. Let me tell you the story of Moses' birth from my perspective, as it is my testimony. This is the story I tell.

I was a Hebrew woman during the time that the Egyptian pharaoh had enslaved my people. Though enslaved, God had blessed the Israelites, and we multiplied greatly. The Egyptians were threatened by our growth and so the Pharaoh ordered that all male babies were to be killed. It was such a scary time to be pregnant. I know this fear well, you see, because I was pregnant with Moses at the time. I did not know if God would bless me with a boy or a girl. Though I must admit, late at night in my own thoughts, I begged God to let it be a girl. Alas though, when he was born, he was a perfect little boy and I loved him so very much. I could not do as the pharaoh ordered, not only because of the love I had for Moses, but also because I loved and feared God. I knew even though the Pharaoh had made the order, he was wrong. What he was asking of us was evil. So, I risked everything, and I hid Moses. It was incredibly difficult to hide him during this time. To begin with, babies need constant attention, but also because we were slaves and forced to work long hours every day. Eventually it came to the point that I could no longer hide my son; I knew I had to do something. I prayed to our Lord and decided to take a basket and coat it with tar and pitch to make it waterproof. I then placed Moses in the basket, placed him among the reeds on the bank of the Nile River and left him in God's hands. Oh, the heartache. A part of my heart broke that day, but it was the only way I knew to keep him safe. I had to trust God would keep him safe.

His sister watched him from afar, and what happened next to my beautiful son was nothing short of a miracle, a blessing from God Himself. I could not believe it at first. When I heard the encounter retold it felt so unreal. God's timing and blessing was impeccable, as always. Moses' sister was the slave to the Pharaoh's daughter. Sometime after I left Moses on the riverbank, the Pharaoh's daughter walked down to the river to bathe. Her servant, Moses' sister, lead her down to the river bank. It was then that the Pharaoh's daughter saw the basket among the reeds. She had her servant fetch the basket and when she opened it, she saw Moses; he was crying, and she felt sorry for my son. The Pharaoh's daughter realized the baby was from one of the Hebrew women. Moses' sister offered to fetch a Hebrew woman to nurse the baby for the Pharaoh's daughter and she agreed. Moses' sister fetched me. God had placed my baby back in my arms, legally this time.

I got to keep him for a while longer, no more did I have to hide him. She even paid me to take care of him, my own son. I could not believe it. My heart was so happy that day. I could not help but praise God for this miracle. So, I nursed Moses until he was old enough to return to the Pharaoh's daughter. Looking back on the day I handed Moses over; it was a bittersweet day. I had to send off my son, for yet a second time and my heart was breaking. I would be handing over a piece of my heart, but I found peace that he was not going to be a slave. He would not live the peasant life that I, his father, his brothers, and sisters lived. He was going to grow up among royalty. And while my heart hurt to hand him over, I knew from experience that God always has a plan. My son lived, I got to keep him longer than I thought I would, and he did not have to be a slave. What I did not know then was the plans God had in store for my son.

Many of you, I am sure, know that Moses grew up to become an amazing tool for God. God used my son, a peasant Hebrew, to free the Israelites from the enslavement the Pharaoh had put us under. Moses was used to begin the journey to the Promised Land. When I look back to that time when I was pregnant with Moses, how scared I was for him. I did not know if I would have a daughter who could live, though would live the life of a slave, or if I would have a son, who would be sought to be killed. When I realized I had a son, a perfect son, I knew I had to be obedient to God, and I could not allow my son to be murdered. How scared I was when I hid him, and then ultimately placed him on the riverbed. I did not know what God would do, but I had faith that He would take care of my son. It was that faith that I clung to; it was my only hope. When God placed him back into my arms, I was speechless. I think back to what if. What if I had not stood up against the Pharaoh's order and risked everything? Where would we be today? I remember though that God works all things out for the good of His people. I could not see how He would work out me giving away my Moses, my sweet son, but He did. Just because I could not comprehend how, did not make it any more unlikely that God would work it out. I just had to trust in Him.

What situations in your life are requiring you to just trust that it will be worked out? Cling to God! Sometimes we are lucky enough to see how God worked it all out. Sometimes, in the case of my son Moses, we do not get to see it all work out in this lifetime. But I have peace knowing Moses got to see it from the other side.

Exodus chapters 1 and 2
Exodus 6:20 (Where we find Jochebed's name)

Jonah

My name is Jonah, and unfortunately many of you have probably heard or read of my cowardliness, my anger, and my unrighteous judgment. Today though, the story I tell is that of a man, a flawed human, much like the ones reading my testimony. I will tell the story of God's grace and mercy, not just for the Ninevites, but also for me.

I am Jonah, the son of Amittai. I was a prophet that served my lord Jeroboam II. Jeroboam II did not delight in the Lord as I did. He still though was successful, for God's mercy was on his chosen people and he saw how everyone in Israel was suffering, both slave and free. God saved them through the hand of Jeroboam. I could hear God's voice and He called me to the capital of Assyria, Nineveh. He called me to preach against them because of their wickedness. I did not want to. What I thought was more adequate instead was for God's immediate justice; to destroy them as justice for their evil ways.

Another prophet named Nahum later spoke of the evilness that came from Nineveh. He said they were a city of blood, lies, lust, prostitutes, uncountable deaths, sorcery, and witchcraft. The evil knew no bounds. In my mind, they were guilty. Their hearts were hardened, and they deserved death; our God did not think so though.

So instead of being obedient to God's word, I ran like the coward I was. I thought I could outrun God's commands. How foolish was I to think I could outrun the calling God had on my life, but I did. I boarded a ship headed for Tarshish, but God had other plans. A violent storm came, and the sailors got scared. They begin to throw the cargo overboard in an attempt to save the ship and their lives. They called out to their own gods with no avail. They went downstairs where I was sleeping.

They cast lots to find out who was responsible for the violent storm and the short lot fell to me. I took the blame and gave God the credit for being the creator of all things. This scared the men further, so I told them to throw me overboard. They did not. They were afraid of what my God would do to them. A part of me just wished they would, so I could drown and be done with this mess I had gotten myself into. Instead, they actually began to cry out to the Lord to save them. You see, what I did not realize then, was that God was using me to share Him with these sailors. God knew I would run; He knew where I would run to, and He knew who I would run into. At the time though, I really just wanted them to throw me overboard so that I did not have to go to Nineveh, and they would get the justice I felt they deserved. Finally, still afraid, and out of options, they threw me overboard. I can admit that I was scared. Death has a funny way of sounding like the better option until you are faced with it.

God though, He was not finished with me yet. After being thrown overboard God provided a huge fish to swallow me whole, and there in the belly of the fish, I called out to the merciful God. Even after my disobedience, even after my anger, He was still listening. He heard my cry. He saved me. From there I set my eyes on His holy temple. After three days and three nights, the huge fish spit me up onto the shore, to the astonishment of the sailors who witnessed the spectacle. God was still using me and my disobedience to help others. I knew then, what I should have known back in the nice comfortability of the kingdom of Jeroboam. I had to preach the words God gave me to Nineveh. It took me three days to walk through the city and I warned them that Nineveh would be overthrown.

Despite hearing Gods word, despite the storm, despite the sailors discovering my God, despite being thrown overboard and swallowed by a fish, despite God saving me inside the belly of the giant fish, despite all of this, my heart STILL held bitterness towards the Ninevites. So, after being obedient and preaching all that God told me to preach, I went and sat down at a place east of the city and stewed in my anger. These people heard my words and repented. But in my mind, I was judge, jury, and executioner. I had decided they were beyond help, guilty, and deserved swift justice; they deserved death. I was angry!!

It was there in that anger I sat in the squelching heat, yet still God provided me a big leaf to provide me shade. He is a God who knows our needs and provides for us. That plant made me happy, that despite my stupidity, disobedience and unrighteousness, God still loved me enough to bless me with that plant. I truly, honestly wish I could at this point tell you that I had learned my lesson, that I understood the correlation between myself and the city of Nineveh, but alas, I did not.

So, the day came and God, knowing I had still not yet fully learned the lesson, provided a scorching wind and blazing sun that withered that plant and in turn withered my relief. I cried out in anger, "Just kill me!!!" I claimed my life would be better if I were just dead. But God reminded me that I had no interest in this plant before, I did not make it, I did not grow it, yet I did not want it to die. How much more does God want for us, His children, that He handmade, grew, and cultivated, to have life in Him. To live and not to die!! I was speechless and humbled. I was so stupid to cast my unrighteous judgment on these people that God loved. He made each of them, just like He had made me. He loved them, just as He loved me. They deserved the same mercy I was given during this time in my life and my future stupid moments that are sure to come.

Jonah 1-4

Hezekiah

Twenty-five years old. I was twenty-five when I became king. I followed behind my father, King Ahaz of Judah. Thankfully, I did not follow in his footsteps. As children, we can either learn how to be, or how not to be, from our parents. For me, I learned how not to live by watching the ways of my father. I guess to fully understand my story, I must first tell you a bit about my biological father. In fact, it is only by God's perfect plan, that I can even tell you my story, or that I even have a story to tell. "My father, King of Judah", those words should elicit pride, but they do not. He might have been king of Judah, a country set apart by God himself for the sake of his servant David, but he had gone the way of the Israelites and gentiles. He worshiped idols as well gods and worse yet, he sacrificed his own children on altars in high places that he had built to Baal. He murdered my own brothers and sister, for what? For nothing!! It could have been me. I dare not say it should have been me though, because it is God's timing, His plan is perfect, and I trust He always knows what He is doing.

I watched my father commit these atrocities, and I learned what not to do. He did not do what was right in the eyes of the Lord, and I knew I did not want any part of that life or lifestyle. Actually, I did not want any part of that certain death, if you will. I set my eyes on my ancestors before me. There were plenty of unrighteousness to learn what not to do, however there were also plenty of righteous men to learn from. My own grandfather, Jotham, was a righteous man who did right in the eyes of the Lord. There were others, too, leading all the way back to King David. My too-many-greats-to-say grandpa was a man who did right in the eyes of the Lord. They were my role models. And when I, at the age of twenty-five became king, the very first thing I set out to do was to undo what my father had done.

In my first month as king, I opened the doors to the temple that my father had shut. I gathered the priest and I acknowledged before them the disastrous effects my father's reigns had on our country. I announced my plans to make a covenant with the Lord, so his anger would turn away from us. I ordered the priests to cleanse themselves and to begin purifying the temple. Every high place, sacred stone, altar, and even Moses' bronze snake, as it had become an idol, had to be destroyed, or cleansed and purified. I ordered sin offerings for the entire kingdom. I ordered thanks offerings, and we participated in Passover.

In everything I did, I did with prayer. Because I did this, the Lord was with me and everything I set out to do. I was successful. I'd like to say that I am not telling you this to brag, but to be honest, pride has always been my downfall. However, leaning on the Lord does make one successful in what they do. If we seek His will, His will becomes our will, and He does not fail. I spent much of my 29 years as king destroying evil things and restoring the holy things. I gave orders and the people respected me, so they did it.

Because the Lord was with me, I had stored up a great deal of wealth. I even had a place built to store the wealth I had accumulated. I am ashamed to admit it, but I began to take pride in how successful I was. This wealth started to become my idol. I had worked hard to destroy the idols my dad and those before him had not only allowed but encouraged. This idol though I did not see coming. It creeped in slowly. God though, He saw it.

At one point I became ill, I was certain to die, but I prayed. Honestly, I begged God to heal me and give me peace. I asked for God to give me a sign that He would heal me. And He did. In my day, we told time by the stairs. The sun moved along the stairs and progressed along as the hours went by. His sign to me was the time on the steps going backwards. It was an impossible miraculous sign. He was faithful, and I was healed.

News of my illness had spread, and the King of Babylon sent envoys to see me. I had been healed and was happy to show them all wealth. I showed it all off to them, every last thing. I failed to mention why I had such wealth. That it was seeking God's will all these years that gave me so much success. My pride, oh my stupid, stupid, pride. I failed to mention the miraculous sign, or the reason for my healing. Why did not I talk about the covenant? Why did not I share how they too could benefit from following the Lord.

Isaiah, the prophet, came to see me after the envoys had left. God knew how prideful I had been. About how stupid I had been. He knew that I had missed the mark and missed my opportunity. Even when Isaiah spoke the prophecy over me, that the Babylonians would take all the treasure we had stored up, that the kingdom would be destroyed, even my own offspring would be taken as eunuchs for the king of Babylon. I knew what the words spoken by Isaiah from the Lord were good and true. But still full of pride, I thought, well at least I will have peace.

You see, I did what was right in the eyes of the Lord. Some have even been known to say there was no other king like me before or after my reign. Even so, I struggled with pride. We all have something we struggle with. We are all stupid, sinful humans. My heart longs to go back in time and do over what I failed to do the first time. I would like to tell of God's goodness, His perfect timing, His love. You see it was the love of David that spared us over the years. As a nation we struggled; we struggled a lot. We had many a righteous king, but we also had many unrighteous kings. They all left their mark, but it was the mercy that God had for David that saved many generations after David. I would like to say that the changes I made lasted forever. That my nation permanently turned away from the idols and worshipping of Baal. It would be a lie though. Take a good look around and you will see that it is still going on. My son, Manasseh, followed behind my reign and became the next King of Judah. I wish I could say that my efforts had at least lasted generations, but my own son, he brought Baal into the temple of the Lord.

Thankfully, we are not judged by God on the acts of our children or of our parents. However, we cannot be foolish and think our actions have no impact on the generations after us. Isaiah's message from the Lord spoke of the ramifications of my pride long after I had left. That will forever be on my name.

2 Kings: 18-20
2 Chronicles 29-32

Loyal Friend

The story I tell, funnily enough, is not really about me. My name is irrelevant. The story I tell is about a man with healing powers, and four of my friends, one of which was paralyzed. We had been hearing stories of this man and how he was traveling around teaching about God and healing the sick. Depending on who you talked to, his work was either a miraculous wonder from God or work of the devil himself. Many though, in my village, thought the latter of his works. For me, the stories about him sparked hope inside of me. Hope for my friend, that he too could be healed and once again walk. Hope that he can return to work and support his family and bring honor to his family.

I knew my friend was a good man, but the shame that came with being unable to support his family had taken a toll on his spirit. He seemed so saddened and helpless. He had lost all hope of being healed. When we began to hear stories of this man's healing, this sense of excitement began to stir in my spirit. I could not help but feel like this was his time, his time to walk again.

We lived in the village of Bethsaida, and the man with healing powers, they called him Jesus of Nazareth, came to our village, and performed many miraculous wonders. He healed and spoke with such authority. However, as I said my village did not see his wonders in the way that I did. They thought of it as evil, and I saw it as hope. Jesus showed contempt for our village. He said woe to Bethsaida, who sees the wonders yet does not repent. I was ready to repent. I was ready to bring my friend to see Jesus of Nazareth, but my friend was not completely ready. He hesitated. It had been so long since he had ever walked, he could not let his mind wander to the prospect that he might walk again. He thought what if Jesus of Nazareth could not heal him, he just could not put himself out there. But I knew Jesus could, I had faith He could. I could feel it deep in my soul. Besides the feeling in my soul, I had seen it for myself.

I had a neighbor, he was blind. Some of his family had taken him to Jesus and they begged Jesus to heal the blind man, to restore his sight. Jesus took him by the hand and led him out of the city. I did not actually see what happened as I did not follow them, but my neighbor never came back. I know in my heart of hearts, he was healed. I do not think he wanted to come back to our village. People around here did not want to believe in Jesus, they did not want to repent. But I was ready, I just had to get my friend to see it too.

So, days passed, and Jesus left our village to continue traveling and I just could not get my paralyzed friend to see that Jesus could heal him. He just had to believe and go with me. So, I stopped trying to convince my friend and instead I gathered three of my other friends and got a plan together. We would conspire to get my friend to Jesus.

Word came that Jesus was in Capernaum, the next village over. So, my three friends and I gathered my friend on a mat and we carried him from Bethsaida to Capernaum. The four of us, carrying our friend, traveled along the sea of Galilee. When we finally reached the village, it was not hard to locate Jesus. The people of Capernaum and surrounding villages had heard that Jesus had come, and they crowded in. Our travel had been long and slow from the four of us carrying our friend, because of that, we were late arriving. The crowd was thick. There was no way to enter the house where Jesus was teaching and healing.

I could see the disappointment on my friend's face. How it changed as his negative thoughts took over. He began to process that he had been right, he would not be healed, he would not walk again. That it was his friend (me) and my false hope that had brought him to this moment of disappointment. He was crushed. I, though, was not ready to throw in the towel. I did not come all this way to quit. I knew, I just knew, Jesus could and would heal my friend. I just had to get him in front of Jesus. As I looked around and inspected the surroundings of this house, I quickly thought of a plan. I climbed the stairs that lead to the roof for repairs and looked around. Yes, my plan would work. I ran back down the stairs to my friends and filled them in. We would lower my friend in from the ceiling.

Ceilings back then were not like they are here in today's world. Our ceilings were made with mud and straw. With a little effort we could dig a hole in the roof. So, the four of us carried him up the stairs. We had to dig a couple of holes before we found where Jesus was in the house, but when we found him, we kept digging until it was big enough to put my friend through. We used the rope we had brought with us and lowered him down on his mat to the feet of Jesus. I was so excited at this point I could barely contain myself. This was the moment I had been working and constantly plotting for. Jesus looked at my friend, He looked up at the four us of peering down at our friend and He saw our faithfulness and He said "Son, your sins are forgiven". Immediately, my friend stood up and began praising God. At that moment he knew too what I had felt all along. Jesus of Nazareth was not doing these signs and teachings from Satan, but from God. He was the son of God. The truly amazing thing was that everyone else saw what Jesus had done for my friend and they too, knew they had seen remarkable things.

I clung to the hope that Jesus could do what I had heard and seen Him do. I was not discouraged by what those around me said. I did not stop when obstacles were placed in my way. It was not always easy; in fact, it would have been easier to quit on my friend. But I knew, in my heart of heart, that Jesus would be faithful too. We did not go back to Bethsaida, I am not sure what would have happened, but if they did not believe it with their own eyes, I do not reckon they would have believed what we had to say either.

Matthew 9:1-8
Matthew 11:21
Mark 2:1-5

Mark 8:22-26
Luke 5:17-20

Thief

In my village, I was known for one thing. They often whispered to each other when I walked through town. "Make sure you secure your things when he is around", they would say. They thought I could not hear them, but I could. They always looked at me suspiciously. Occasionally I even saw fear in their eyes. I was given titles such as thief, rebel, and criminal. Though if I were to be honest, I was. I was all those things. I found pleasure in stealing and why shouldn't I? I did not have to work hard like the other men. I just took what I wanted when I wanted it. And I was good at it. They all "knew" I was a thief; they just had not caught me yet. Well, that was until that fateful day.

There was all this commotion going on around the village. There was talk about a man named Jesus of Nazareth that was performing signs and wonders. Some people wanted to see the wonders; some just wanted him dead. I knew what it felt like to be hated by society, so I wanted to see him for myself. Once I got there and saw the crowd surrounding him, I realized how easy it would be to steal from all these unsuspecting people. So that is what I did. I went around stealing right from their baskets. It was like fishing from a barrel, criminally easy.

It was as I was reaching in to steal the gold right out of a satchel of a Pharisee that I spotted the man we had all come to see. For a split second our eyes locked onto each other. There was just something about him. The way he spoke mesmerized me. There I was stuck in motion, my hand in the pharisees satchel, jaw dropped, ears tuned in. It was like there was no one around except me and this man they called Jesus. That was until this loud yelling and commotion going on around me jolted me back to the real world. It was then that I realized the commotion was coming from the man who satchel my hand was still in. And before I even realized it, a Roman guard had a chain on my other wrist.

There it was, they always had suspicion, but now I had been caught red-handed. It wasn't just that my hand was in the other man's satchel, but that my own satchel was filled with all the loot I had stolen from the crowd. There was no denying my guilt. No lie that could get me out of trouble now. I was hauled off to jail to await my sentencing. Little did I know, the man who had captivated me and ultimately was the catalyst for my capture, it wasn't the last time I'd see him. Boy am I glad about that.

Remember how I said some people wanted the man named Jesus dead? Well, they had been pushing and pushing for that, and were well on their way to accomplishing it. To my surprise, when I was brought from the jail to hang on my cross, Jesus was there on his own. There I was, then Jesus, and then a competitor of mine, another thief. I could not understand though why Jesus was there hanging with us. The crowd was so incredibly rude. They taunted Jesus, they called Him names, they spat on Him and ridiculed Him, but for what? They had not even a reason to charge Him, much less crucify Him. Even the thief hanging on the other side of Jesus taunted him "saying if you really are the Messiah then save yourself and us" I thought how ridiculously selfish. We had done the deeds they charged us with, we deserved the death they sentenced us with, but He, Jesus, He did not. He was an innocent man.

I did not fully understand what was going on with this man called Jesus. They called him the Messiah, they called him King of the Jews, but it was all fuzzy for me. Those names really did not mean much to me. What I did know was, this man was innocent. Pilate himself even said so. What else I noticed, was that He did not react like other people did. He did not proclaim his innocence, He did not react in anger, He did not curse at them, He took it, He accepted it. And that was the moment I realized there was more to this man then met the eye, that was beyond all comprehension. He said "Father, forgive them, for they do not know what they are doing". I remember those words exactly how He had spoken to them. Who was this father He was talking to. And on the cross, being ridiculed and treated like the scum of the earth, He asked for forgiveness, not for Himself, but for those treating Him this way. I did not know where He came from, who this father was, but I knew I wanted to live like Him, and I wanted to be with Him. I said "Jesus, remember me when you come into your kingdom". Jesus's response to me was so powerful, I no longer feared my imminent death that was moments away. I felt a peace come over me like I had never felt before. He said, "Truly I tell you, today you will be in paradise."

Mark 15: 25-32
Luke 23:32-43

Rahab

Shame, it's an emotion I have felt many times over the years. I have had to remind myself time and time again that God's grace is enough. God delivered me and my entire family from the life I used to live. He set me free of that life filled with shame. I want to tell you about God's goodness, but to do so, I must first tell you of my past. The past that brings me shame.

My name is Rahab, and I lived in Jericho. My house was built into the wall that surrounded the village. Just a few yards away from being a literal outcast of my village. The location of my house was perfect for my profession, if you want to call it that. My house being built in the wall of the village allowed travelers to easily access me for favors. I was a prostitute and an inn keeper; my customers were foreigners and villagers alike. While the house was good for my profession, it also made me incredibly vulnerable if Jericho were ever invaded. The reality of such an event was pressing upon us as the rumors circulated that the Israelites would soon be invading Jericho. The entire village had this thick feeling of fear over it, and I was not exempt.

Along with the rumors of war, there were stories about the God of the Israelite people. We had heard about how their Lord had dried up the Red Sea and how they had been able to completely destroy Sihon and Og. They had been told that the Lord was giving the Israelites their land, the land we lived on. The God they believed, was a God I felt was worth trusting in. I did have fear, but one night when two Israelites came to my house, I knew this was my chance to put my faith into action.

One evening two Israelites stopped to rest at my house. The king of Jericho had heard that spies had come to get intel on Jericho. I quickly took the men to the roof and hid them under the stalks of flax. When the messenger came to tell me, the men had been spies, I lied to them. I told them the men had already left before the gates closed at dusk. I told them to hurry, they still might be able to catch them. So, they ran off in that direction to catch the spies. After the messengers were long gone, I went back up to the roof top. I told the men that I knew who they were. I told them that I had lied to the messengers and in doing so I risked my life. In return I asked them to show my family kindness and to give me a sign that they would not kill myself or my family. The men agreed. They instructed me to not let any of my family leave, because they could not guarantee their safety if they did. The sign to the army would be a scarlet rope tied to the window. The very rope that I let down for them to escape. When they returned, the scarlet rope would be the signal to the army to not to harm anyone in the house.

Eventually the Israelites came and took the land we knew as Jericho. The Israelites had honored our agreement. My entire family was safe. From that point on, their God was my God. A God of grace and mercy, a God of power and strength. In hindsight I can see the thumbprints on how God brought all this about. God led them to my house. He gave me the courage to lie to the king's messenger. This alone could have cost me my life if they had discovered I had lied. God's love and compassion saved me, a Canaanite living in a country that He was giving to the Israelites, by allowing me to help them. It was an unlikely combination, but then again God works in the unlikely. He knew my heart, and my openness to Him.

After saving my family, God gave me a son name Boaz. Boaz came to be a great man of his word, doing right by other people. He was a compassionate, successful businessman. A son to be proud of. If I had not been a prostitute living in the wall of Jericho that made an easy cover for the Israelites, had He not given me courage, had He not used honorable men to be the spies and keep their word, I would not be here to tell you my story. Boaz's story would not have existed. It is an intricate web He weaves, and I am so thankful for His master plan.

Joshua 2

Joshua 6:22-23
Ruth 4

Nehemiah

My people are of the people of Israel. My home is Jerusalem. We had been a wicked nation that turned away from God's commands. Because of that, God did as He said He would. He scattered us among the nations. It was because of the word that said if we turned back to Him, if we repented and pleaded with Him, that He would forgive all our offenses. Our captors in the new nations would have mercy on us. It was because of this word, and holding onto the truth in it, that I Nehemiah, a cup bearer to the king, was able to walk through the door that God opened though King Artaxerxes.

One evening, in the month of Nisan, when bringing him wine, the king had asked me why I looked sad all the time. I was very much afraid, but I answered him with my own question. I asked, "Why should I not be sad when the city where my ancestors are buried lies in ruins and its gates have been destroyed by fire?" And the king asked me "What is it that you want?" In that moment I realized the word was being fulfilled. My captor, my master, was having mercy on me. God had heard my prayer; He heard my plea for forgiveness, and He had forgiven all my offenses. Not only that, but God had used my captor to open the door to fulfill the desire He had laid on my heart.

When it pleased the King to send me, I also bravely asked him to provide me with papers for safe travel and timber to restore my land. Because God's gracious hand was on me, the King granted my requests. I did not tell anyone the desires God had laid on my heart, but I gathered my people and led them. We began to restore the gates to Jerusalem and the wall that surrounded it. It had been destroyed by fire and had never been restored. It was a disgrace to our land and to our people. Even when we were mocked by the surrounding countries, even when they said I was rebelling against the king, I did not let them discourage me. I told them the hand of God was upon us, and that as His servants, we would be successful.

As we began rebuilding the sheep gate, the fish gate, the dung gate, the valley gate, the towers, and the wall that surrounded all of Jerusalem, we made sure to dedicate each part. God had his hand upon us. We wanted to give it all to Him. To praise Him and lift up our work in His name. Some of the nobles from tribes could not be bothered to work, but we pressed on without them. Men of all skills joined together to complete the work. We were united, despite any differences we had, for one task: to restore Jerusalem.

As we continued building, more and more ridicule came our way. Anger filled those countries around us. Time after time they tried to attack us, distract us, fill us with fear and get us to quit and ultimately destroy us. Every attack was met with our giving prayer to God for wisdom to see past their fear tactics. We worked with one hand, armed with a weapon in the other. We were always on guard; at one point we were either guarding the backs of our brothers or we were working. God took care of every attempt to destroy us. He was upon us and had given us success.

After the city walls were restored, we restored Jerusalem itself. We put in place gatekeepers, guards, musicians, commanders, Levites, and set rules to keep us safe. The men of Israel retuned to occupy Jerusalem. The word was fully restored. The captors of many nations showed grace and tens of thousands returned home from exile.

When I had first returned to Jerusalem, it was evident that not only did the walls need restored, but the broken people needed restored too. That though, is not my story to tell, I will leave that up to my dear friend Ezra. My hope is that my story will bring a reminder that God lays desires on your heart for a purpose. The desire is not for us to long for and never do anything with it. The desire is there to drive us to move forward with His plan. It is also a reminder that if He puts the desire in your heart, He will open doors that you are not expecting Him to open. Even doors you did not knock on. I did not approach King Artaxerxes on my own. I did not create this master plan to persuade him to go along with my plan. God opened his eyes to see my heartache and he asked me a question that opened a door for me to walk through to begin the process of walking out the desires God had placed on my heart. One final reminder I want to leave you with; if God lays a desire on your heart for a purpose, He will make sure to equip you with the tools you will need to complete the task. Do not worry about how you will do this, say ok Lord, I am willing what's next. God does not call the qualified, He qualifies the called. Take each step in faith that the next step will be there. I promise you the reward will be a blessing far beyond your wildest dreams.

1 Kings 8:46-51
Nehemiah 1-7

Rhoda

My name is Rhoda, and I am sure most of you are thinking who is Rhoda? Honestly though, that is ok. The story I tell is not about how God saved me, though He did. Our story to tell is not always about how I once was and how I now am. Those are great stories, but sometimes our stories are about how we witnessed God's work, even in others' lives. Your eyewitness testimony is also your story. What you have seen, how you felt, how it changed your life, all of that is the story you tell. So here is the story I tell.

My story takes place about 40 years or so after Jesus had died. Peter was traveling around preaching and teaching the gospel to both Jews and gentiles alike. King Herod was in command and came from a long line of Roman men and woman who had slaughtered many over their Christian faith. His grandfather was the one who had ordered all male babies to be murdered in an attempt to kill the baby Jesus. His sister Hernias was the one responsible for the beheading of John the Baptist. Needless to say, this family was ruthless.

During this time, King Herod had arrested some that belonged to the church, intending to persecute them. James, one of the original twelve disciples of Jesus, was captured and was martyred with a sword. King Herod saw the Jews approved of this, so he sought to do it again. Motivated by his pride, he had Peter, another of Jesus's disciples arrested, fully intending to have him put to death as well.

I was gathered with a great many other people at the house of my servant Mary, the mother of both James, who had been martyred, and John Mark. The house was filled with what I can only describe as mourning expectation. My master Mary had lost her son, but had lost him as he stood strong in his faith. Such sadness and pride all at the same time. Also pressing at that moment was the fate of Peter. We were gathered as a group, praying for God's supernatural escape for Peter. We knew that the trial in the morning would mean certain death. The same death that fell upon James, was most certain to fall upon Peter in just hours. We had prayed for James, but still yet his death had come. This was fresh on our minds. We had seen Jesus do mighty things while He walked the earth and even after His death. We knew that He could still do mighty things, so we continued praying individually yet united in our prayers.

It was during that time that I heard a knock on the door. As the servant of the house, it was my job to answer it. So, I went to the door, calling out asking who was there. I did not dare open the door anymore, unless I knew who was standing on the other side. The Roman soldiers were arresting people for simply being associated with the church. If they were going to arrest us, they would have to work harder. I was not about to open the door and make it easy on them. When, I called out asking who it was. He replied it was Peter. My entire spirit and body got so excited. I recognized his voice; he was who he said he was. I got so excited I ran to tell the others. Peter is at the door; Peter is at the door!!! They did not believe me though because I actually hadn't let him in. They thought I was foolish to believe that he was actually at the door!!

I kept insisting that he was actually at the door. Some believed me that I had heard him at the door, but thought that it was probably just his angel. Peter kept knocking. Eventually I got them to the door, and they saw it truly was him. We all burst out with excitement, but Peter had motioned for us to be quiet. He then told us all that had occurred that night. Peter told about how an angel had come and kicked his side as he slept between two soldiers. How he had gotten dressed, and the shackles just fell off his hands and feet. He followed the angel as they passed by guards, who did not even notice them. He told us how the gates just opened themselves. Then when he was outside and had walked the length of one street the angel disappeared. He knew without a doubt that the Lord had sent that angel to save him from certain execution.

That night Peter had left us just as quickly as he showed up. That night our prayers had been answered beyond our comprehension. So far beyond our comprehension that it took time to register in our minds, simply because it was not in the realm of possibility. We knew we had been asking God to do the impossible, so why were we so shocked and slow to believe it when He was faithful? God is still in the business of answering prayers and performing miracles, even after Jesus no longer walks the earth. We cannot stop praying for them simply because we cannot comprehend what He can do. We cannot let our realm of plausibility limit our prayer life. We also must never forget the power of individual prayer united together for one purpose.

Acts 12:1-17
Mark 6:14-29
Matthew 2:13-18

Simon of Cyrene

I had traveled from Cyrene to Jerusalem for the Passover celebration. I was reignited with joy and peace as I began the long journey back to my home in Cyrene. There is just something about taking the time to undergo purification ahead of Passover, and then joining in fellowship with likeminded people over food, which reminds us of our freedom and what our forefathers did for us. Most importantly though, is what our Father in Heaven has done for us. That excitedly content feeling just burns deep into your soul. I was very thankful to be able to make the journey to participate in Passover that year.

As I began my journey back home, I had no way of knowing what was in store for me. As I was walking, my thoughts of how good our Lord is, was disrupted as up ahead there was a loud commotion. I ran ahead to see what was the matter. There before me stood a group of Roman soldiers and three men with crosses. I instantly knew these men were headed out of the city walls to be crucified. One of the men though looked far worse than the other two. He was on his knees hunched over. The only thing keeping him from being completely on the ground was the cross. He was hunched over the top of the cross, it bearing his full weight. There was blood dripping down his face from what appeared to be a crown of thorns. The Roman soldiers were kicking him and mocking his inability to carry the cross any further. They were so entrenched in their ridicule of this man that they did not even notice that I had come upon them.

I could not handle what they were doing to him. I did not even know him, but my heart hurt for him. I yelled out, "Stop! What are you doing? You are going to crucify him; must you humiliate him to the point he cannot even stand much less carry the cross you burdened him with?" As I was calling these men out for their awful actions, the man on the ground, with more effort than it should have been, lifted his head ever slightly and our eyes locked on each other. It was in that moment, that I realized this beaten, swollen man was not a stranger to me, it was Jesus of Nazareth. I had seen Him teach and perform miracles; I knew in my heart that He had to be the Son of God. It felt like my heart stopped beating. I could not breathe. I did not stumble across Roman soldiers humiliating a criminal just to get their kicks off before crucifying him. This was an innocent man. But just as quickly as I was overcome with an array of emotions from fear, anger, and sadness, this peace came over me. I broke eye contact from Jesus when the Roman soldiers started pushing me from behind. They were yelling, "if you have so much compassion for this man, then you help Him carry his cross". The Roman soldiers forced me to carry the cross, to participate in the crucifixion of an innocent man. I gently helped Jesus up off the ground, tears flowing down my face, I lifted the top the cross and we began moving on towards Golgotha where the murder would take place.

A murder was all I could call it. Crucifixion was what we called the judgment for criminals, but He was no criminal. With each step I took my tears turned to sobs, I could not help but feel like I was helping these Roman soldiers carry out this atrocity. As we were walking though, Jesus put His hand only my shoulder for strength to help Him continue the walk. The moment He touched my shoulder my heart felt different, my mind started to think differently. I had heard that Jesus told his disciples that He must go to Jerusalem to be handed over to the chief priest and die. That very moment, I realized what was happening. I was not participating in the Roman soldiers or chief priest's plan, but God's plan. I was being the strength that Jesus needed me to be. I was not helping the soldiers; I was helping Jesus. From that moment until we got to Golgotha, I stood with my shoulders strong, Jesus did not say anything to me, He did not have the strength. Honestly, He did not even need to speak. Our hearts so close together, spoke more than words ever could have.

Once we arrived at the place of the skull, the soldiers made me leave the area. I went to where a group of women were gathered in the distance. They had come from Galilee and were prepared to care for Jesus's needs in death. From noon until three that day in the brightness of daylight, during the crucifixion of Jesus, it went dark. We were in the distance and could not tell what exactly was going on, but there was commotion among the soldiers and the ground shook and rocks split open. Jesus had died and the earth was reacting. My heart was broken. I did not know Jesus long, I did not know a lot about Him, but my heart longed to be close to Him again; to get to know Him more. I resumed my travels home shortly after that. I could not wait to get home to my sons, Alexander and Rufus. I wanted to tell them of everything I had seen. About Jesus. That I was confident He was different than anyone we had ever met. I wanted to tell them in my heart of hearts, I knew He was the Son of God. I could not really explain it, but I also knew that one day I would see Him again. I am actually looking forward to that day.

Matthew 27:32-50
Mark 15:21-22
Luke 23:26-31

Widow of Juppa

I really wish I could show you the robe I hold tight to myself. You might call it drab with its plain cream color. You might call it simple because it does not have the ornate trim of the ones king's wear. You might call it worn out with the stains of years passed that had left their mark on it. You might even call it worthless or trash, and to a degree you might be right. To me though, this robe represents the love of my dear friend Dorcas. To me it represents goodness and a humble spirit. This really is not my story to tell, but Tabitha, as she was known to some, in her humble spirit will not tell the story.

I could tell you the end without the beginning, but what good would that be? Who likes half a story? So, let's begin, at the beginning. I have lived in Joppa my whole life. I was married to a captain of a ship that transported goods out of the ports of Joppa. I met my husband one day down at the ports. I had been going to purchase some fish for my family. He was such a rugged man with a beard and brown eyes. He did not have the best language, but he was so incredibly kind to me. My family did not like him. They said sailing ships was dangerous and not a proper way to provide for a family. They said I needed to marry the landowner from across the way, that they had already arranged it. They said farming would be a steady way to provide for a family, and that I would live close by still. I could not marry that landowner. He was a brute of a man, treated me poorly, like I was one of his cattle. He did not speak the nice words to me that my love did. So, the night before my wedding ceremony to the landowner, I left my father's house with only the clothes I had on. I made my way to the ports, and I found my love before he left for a trip. He had a small house near the ports, I guess many would have called it a shack. I stayed there while he was away. We found a crooked priest who was willing to marry us for a sum of money. My love took care of it all for me. I wish I could say this story ended with, "and we lived happily ever after;" but alas it did not.

We had not been married but for a couple of months. It was hard when he left on his trips, but I was getting used to it. I knew this was how he made his living. I knew I should be grateful for the income, but sometimes it was just so hard. My parents knew it would be hard, it was why they forbade me from marrying him. But young love knows no logic. I knew I loved him; I still do. If I had the chance to do it over again, I think I would do it all the same. Call me foolish, call me stupid, but I loved him so. Not seeing my family compounded the loneliness of my heart. I had not seen them since that fateful night when I chose to run. I knew I could never show my face around there again. I had cost my family too much financially. I knew I broke my mother's heart. For that I am truly sorry. Perhaps there was a better way, a way to get what we both wanted, but I could not see it, then or now.

So that evening when he set out on his third trip since we had been married, I hugged him, kissed him, and promised him I would be ok while he was away. We knew the approximate date he would return, but we never knew exactly, as weather always played an unpredictable role in his timing. I told him I would be waiting at the port for him when he arrived. He stole another kiss as he ran off to load the ship. I watched from the shore as they did their safety checks and pushed off. I remained strong until they pushed off. Then the tears started flowing down my cheeks. I already missed him so much. I knew without a doubt that he missed me too. He was my best friend, and I was his. What we had, did not come around often. In my world, women were bartered as property for marriage. We did not date until we found the one. Had I not been where was when I was buying fish, had he not been in from the sea at the same time, perhaps we would have never met, never fall in love, and never would have married against the protests of everyone in my life. If we had not married, I most definitely would not have met my dear friend, Dorcas. I would not have learned all the amazing things she shared with me. But I guess

I am getting the cart in front of the horse now, so let me back up.

We knew his trip should take nine days with the best weather, longer if the storms did not stay away. The weather had been perfect here that week, so early on the morning as the sun rose, I went down to the ports to wait for my love to come home. The sun was shining bright that hot day, but breeze off the water made it very comfortable. I waited under a tree that looked over the ports. I would be able to see him as he came in. I would run down to greet him as he unloaded. As dusk came, I was sad to not see him, but I was not worried. The weather was nice here, but that did not mean it was nice elsewhere. As dusk turned to night, I headed home to our little house. I knew he would not arrive at night. He always timed his arrivals so the merchants could unload their goods the same day. That way he did not have to work the next day so we could spend all our time together. The next morning, I was back under the tree waiting for his arrival. Another day went by, and he did not arrive. The pit in my stomach began to form, but it was still so early. He said it would be 9-12 days and today was only day ten. Still though, I could not shake the sinking feeling in my belly.

Day ten turned to eleven, day eleven to twelve, and continued in this way. The men coming off the ships told stories of a big storm that had come over the sea. With each passing man came a bigger more extravagant story than the next. You honestly did not know what was fact and what was a fisherman's tale. The one thing that remained consistent, every man said we were lucky to get away with our lives. Each night I cried myself to sleep. In the short time my love and I had, I had not provided him with a baby, now though I was glad. What would I have done alone with such despair and having to care for a child? At the same time, I wished I had had a child, so a part of my love could be with me. Each passing day the reality beat at my door that he was not coming back, but I refused to believe it. It was not until there was no food left that I had to face the reality. He nor his shipmates or ship had been seen since the day we said goodbye. The reality, as much as I tried to deny it, was that I was a widow. A widow, just months after being married. A widow with no family to help me survive. If I was going to survive, I had to find a suitor willing to marry a young widow, who was no longer a virgin. I could not do that to my love. I could not marry another young man. To do so would be to give up all hope that he would return, it would be to acknowledge the sea he loved had devoured him. So, I made the only choice my heart had left to make, I chose not to survive. I sat down under the tree I had sat at for what seemed like years now, though it was barely weeks. I decided I would die in this spot waiting for him to arrive, so somehow the world would know I did not give up on my love.

It was under this tree that I met Dorcas. My sweet, sweet Dorcas. She had seen me under this tree, pitifully dirty and starving. The only clean part of my body was my cheeks where the tears continued to shower them on a daily basis. Somehow, she knew my heartache. Somehow, she recognized the pain for what it was. She was a kindred heart for my widow heart. She held my hand and whispered, "come with me." I did not know what to do, I did not want to leave my post, but I had no argument left in me. She helped lift me up off the ground, as I did not have the energy or the desire to muster it myself. She led me back to her house. She fed me the first real meal I had had since I ran out of food in our house a week or so before. She had clean water for me to drink. She never left my side, her hand in my hand. Somehow her hand was radiating energy into my hand, into my heart. After eating, she helped me to bathe and dressed me in this robe, her robe, which became my robe. That night I slept in the robe, snuggled tightly against me. I slept better than I had in weeks. I slept like I used to, with my love by my side. I know this sounds crazy, but the love she poured into making that robe was tangible. I could feel it enclose me. It did not take the place of my husband, but that robe made the ache a little less.

I was not the first widow Dorcas had made a robe for nor was I the last. After those first days, Dorcas began to tell me about her beliefs. I was a gentile and had never heard the things she told me. She talked about the love of a man she had heard of named Jesus, that she believed He was the Messiah, about God and His saving grace. I did not think I could ever have forgiveness after leaving my family. What Dorcas taught me gave me so much peace. My heart still misses my love, and I know I will never marry again, but it's unexplainable the comfort I have now. The comfort of this robe and the single act of how it came to be, is beyond comprehension. As my healing began, and my strength returned, I began to help Dorcas and her mission of taking care of the widows. Showing them the same love she showed me. The love of Jesus.

Years and many widows later, Dorcas became ill and died. My heart hurt so much. We prepared her for death and placed her in an upstairs room. We gave her body, even after death, the respect she deserved. The disciples of Jesus, the very man Dorcas had taken time to teach me about, heard that Peter, another disciple was in Lydda. It was not far from us, so they sent two men to Peter and urged him to come at once. When Peter arrived, we told him of the goodness of Dorcas. The Jewish widows spoke of Tabatha, but to me she will always be Dorcas. We showed him all the robes she had made with love for us. We spoke through tears of all the ways she had cared for us and the poor. She was an amazing woman of God. She might have passed on, but her love was just as tangible then as it was when she was alive.

Peter asked everyone to leave. I am not sure what happened during that time. The widows that believed in God, we gathered and prayed for Peter as he went upstairs. We did not really know what we should be praying for. The fact was, Dorcas was dead. We prayed that God would be with Peter when he was with Dorcas. A little while later, Peter called for the believers, making sure all the widows who were believers had space in the room. He presented Dorcas, alive. We stood there stunned, shocked and a bit in disbelief. How was this possible? How…How…and then it finally hit us, she is alive! We all immediately started crying and screaming in delight as we all hugged and just lived in this moment of joy. The news spread all over Joppa and many people believed in the Lord.

As I touched on before, if I had not been buying fish, if my love had been out to sea, and though it still hurts, if my love had not been lost at sea, if Dorcas had not found me under that tree, my life would not be the life I live today. I have learned through Dorcas and the disciples, including Peter as he stayed behind in Joppa preaching and teaching after the miracle he performed with my Dorcas. God was orchestrating my life before I even knew Him. He loved me, before I knew Him. I was made in His image. He knew where I would be at every stage in my life, even when my choices were stupid. Even when I chose to give up this very life He breathed, He had a plan. Dorcas was His plan. He laid on her heart to help the widows, she helped many including me. Over the years I have also come to learn, this widow of a captain was also His plan.

Acts 9:36-42

Aquila & Priscilla

My wife, Priscilla and I, Aquila, were no strangers to persecution. We were Jews from Pontus but had been living in Italy. Back home in Pontus, was our family, but we felt pressed to leave home to travel to Italy to help take care of Christians that had been scattered there during persecution. I was a tent maker and it meant I could do my trade anywhere. Unlike fisherman, I did not need to live in any particular location. Everyone needed tents, and I could carry my tools wherever I went. We worked alongside some of the most well-known missionaries in our time, I am sure you knew them, Paul and Timothy to name a few. You probably had not heard much about my wife and I; we preferred it that way. We worked behind the scenes. It really is not like us to tell our story, but we hope it will be an encouragement to others who work behind the scenes. Your work is just as valuable as those in the limelight.

It was during the time before our good friend Paul had been blinded by the Lord and came to a saving relationship with Jesus. He was a religious zealot, taught by the top Pharisees. His direct persecution of Christians caused many to flee for their lives. coincidently this caused the good news of Jesus Christ to spread further and further. My wife and I had been talking about the poor families that were fleeing, leaving behind their homes and security. I realized, as tentmaker, that I had the ability to help those families. It was then, that my wife and I decided to willingly leave the comfort of our own home and security to move to Italy to give these families, many with little children, a sense of security through shelter. I made them new homes with my tents.

We met many people during this great persecution. We met fisherman, farmers, tax collectors, prostitutes, widows, beggars, and orphans. We met believers and nonbelievers. We told stories to the young, and listened to the elderly as they trusted us with their memories. We laughed with them. We cried with them. We worked alongside them in their fields. We ate alongside them at the tables.

It was while we were in Italy, living among the Christians there, that persecution also broke out there. Claudius, the commander, had ordered all the Jews to leave Rome. The Jewish lifestyle became a threat to the Roman kingdom. We did not worship the Roman kings, and therefore we needed to be removed from the land. He ordered all Jews to leave Rome, so we headed for Corinth. In Corinth, we did the same as we had in Italy. We worked alongside the Christians there. We built a tent and welcomed them into our home, and we helped build other tents for those who had to leave their home in Italy behind.

It was there, working in Corinth, that we met our dear friend Paul. By this time Paul, who was also known as Saul, had an encounter with God. In Damascus, he had been blinded by the sight of God. He was blind for 3 days until a prophet named Ananias healed him after receiving a message from the Lord to find Paul. After Paul's encounter he was a changed man. He used the knowledge he had gained from studying under the top Pharisees and his experiences with God and the apostles to share the good news about Jesus Christ and what it meant for us. Talk about a one-eighty, he went from being a religious zealot to being on fire for Jesus.

Paul was also a skilled worker and he joined alongside us in our work while also preaching and teaching in the community. He was winning hearts by sharing the news about what Jesus had done for us. It was an amazing thing to see. Paul stayed in Corinth for 18 months. During that time our friendship and bond was strengthened from working, eating, praying, and worshipping together. We also witnessed the miracles of God opening hearts together and working miracles through his disciples. So, when the time came for Paul to move on, and he asked us to join him on his mission, we agreed wholeheartedly. What God was doing through our team, we could not deny. Even if it meant leaving everything behind again. So, the three of us set sail for Syria. We decided to stop at Ephesus. Paul was able to reason with the Jews in the synagogue, but it was in the community that we realized how much help they needed. They needed our hospitality. There were many widows and orphans there. Our hearts went out to the them. We knew we had to stay.

The people of Ephesus begged Paul to stay, but he declined. If I am honest, my wife and I longed for him to stay too. We knew though, that we were all doing God's work, not our own. Just as our mission was here in Ephesus, Paul's missions carried him all over. God called him where he was to go, and he went. From Ephesus Paul set sail for Caesarea. He did promise to come back though if it was God's will. From that moment on we were no longer in the same mission field, yet we always covered him in our prayers. We supported him the best we could, while still doing what we were called to do. You see, Paul's mission of teaching, reasoning, preaching, was no more or less important than our mission of hospitality and prayer. Together we worked to accomplish God's plan. Together we planted seeds, nourished seeds, and harvested. Without Paul or without my wife and I, without you and your cog in the mission, it would not be the same or as effective. What is your ministry? Looking back how has God used you alone and in conjunction with others?

Acts 18:1-20
Romans 16:3-5
1 Corinthians 16:19
2 Timothy 4:19

The Woman at the Well

It was so hot outside. The sun front and center in the sky, beating down on any and everything. It had no mercy for those willing to be out. The wind blew slightly, and the dust blew along with it. At the noon hour, no person in their right mind would be outside. That was me, not in my right mind, out there in the middle of the day in the peak of the heat. I was headed to the well to get water. I didn't want to do it, but my thirst won out. I couldn't dare go out when the other women did, once the sun began to go down, and shade offered some relief from the sun.

To say I wasn't welcome among the other ladies, would be an underestimate. They didn't just talk about me, it was the looks they gave me, the way they tried to hide their sons if ever we were near each other. To be honest, I wasn't welcome by anyone in my village. I burned more bridges than I could count. My actions, had brought me to this point, gathering water, in the heat of the day, to avoid the looks, the muttered words, the shaming and outcasting.

My word was no longer of value, because my decisions contradicted whatever my word might have said. I slept around with many of the men in this town. Young or old, married or single, it didn't really matter to me. I had been married five times before, a disgrace enough to warrant disdain from the village, but that wasn't the worst of it. I was then laying down with a man that wasn't one of the five, we were not married. This, the woman could not forgive. They didn't me around their family. So, there I was headed to the well, a temporarily deserted place. As I walked up, I saw what could not be. My eyes must have been playing a trick on me, because I thought I saw a man sitting at the well. As I slowly walked up, for a moment I thought about returning home. I didn't want to face a mocker, my heart wasn't up for it. Men though, they were my weakness and so I decided to keep going. As I arrived at the well, the man asked me for a drink. I realized he was a Jew. Was I dreaming, a Jewish man, asking me to get him some water? This was not allowed, he really shouldn't even be talking to me.

In that moment, I didn't know what I know now. But in that moment, I could tell there was something different in this man. I didn't know what it was, but I could feel it. And then he started speaking in what I could only describe as riddles. He said If I knew the gift of God, and who this man was that was asking me for a drink, that I would ask him, and he would have given me water. I was so confused. This man had nothing to draw water from the well. Even in this confusion, I didn't get frustrated with him. I knew he wasn't mocking me, like the people from my village often did. Then he told me about the spring of water welling up to eternal life. He talked about how one would never be thirsty again if they drank from this spring, versus the water that was in the well. I wanted that water. In that moment, I thought, surely if this man gave me a drink of this spring water he speaks of then, I wouldn't have to come out in the high noon heat. Looking back, I was foolishly confused and didn't realize what this man was actually offering me.

So, he told me to go and call on my husband and come back to the well. I hung my head, and I muttered the words, that I was certain would bring about mocking that those in my village were so inclined to heap on me. I whispered, I have no husband. It was then, that this stranger, whom I had never met, and he had never met me before, told me all about myself. He knew of not just the man I was laying with out of wedlock, but he knew my past of my five husbands!! I knew he must be a prophet. I talked about my ancestors who worshiped on the mountain, and I tried to shift my blame on not worshipping because the Jews claimed we have to be in Jerusalem to worship. This prophet though, he spoke of future events of worship and he spoke about how us Samaritans worshiped what we did not know. He said "Yet a time is coming and has now come when the true worshipers will worship the Father in the Spirit and in truth, for they are the kind of worshipers the

Father seeks. God is spirit and his worshipers must worship in the Spirit and in truth". I do not have words to explain how I felt in that moment, but I wanted to be a part of what it was he spoke of. Because though I could not explain it, I said the only thing I did know. I said, I know that the Messiah is coming, and when He comes, He will explain everything to us. The next words out of his mouth were "I, the one speaking to you-I am He". I stood there speechless. I saw a group of men walking toward us and for a moment I was frozen in time. Then, as thunder comes after lightening, slightly delayed, it hit me. This man was not a prophet, He must be who He said he was. He was the Messiah.

I couldn't delay, I didn't even take my water jar with me. I went back to the village and said to people, "Come, see a man who told me everything I ever did" Could this really be the Messiah? He surely had to be. You know the most puzzling thing of all to me, was that people believed me. My word had been so far tarnished, but for some reason, they believed me. Why did the Messiah, chose to meet me, the self-destroyed, tarnished Samaritan? Whatever His reasoning, it worked, because many of the villagers believed because of my words, and they too wanted to meet Him. If I can depart any words on you, it is this, if God can use me, He can use you too.

John 4:1-30 & 39-42

Cornelius

A centurion, a roman commander of 100 men. That is how I was known among the people. I was more than a commander though, I was also a father, a husband and people say I was generous to the poor. The way I saw it, I was just doing what I thought anyone who was able to would do. I was a gentile living in Caesarea among Jews. Rome had taken over the land and we were stationed around the country to help maintain peace in the land. From the Jews I had heard about God. I did not know a lot about Him, but over time I was able to gather information from having conversations with the Jews. I was well respected among the Jews; I treated them how I would want to be treated. I made sure my men did too. They might be a little different than me, but they still had a heart and feelings just like everyone else. And the God they taught me about, I feared Him, but I wasn't scared of Him. I feared Him, much like my children feared me, they respected me, they loved me. It was the same way with their God. So, I prayed to God regularly and I sought to know more and more about Him.

One day while stationed in Caesarea after eating lunch in my house, I began to spend time in prayer. I knew the Jews prayed three times a day and I tried to make sure I did too. I am unsure if it was while I was praying or after I was praying, but around three in the afternoon I had a vision. I remember the vision as clearly today as if it were yesterday. A man in shining clothes stood before me. I thought, "am I dreaming? Is this real?" And the man said, "Cornelius." He knew my name!! This could be no other but the Lord, or a messenger of the Lord. I stood for what was probably a second, but felt like forever. I was so startled and shocked. Finally, I responded "What is it, Lord?" The man said he had heard my prayers and how I had given and supported those less fortunate, had been accepted as a memorial offering to God. From this I knew the man was not God, but a messenger of God. He told me to send men to

Joppa, to bring back a man named Simon who is called Peter. He said he was staying with Simon the tanner by the sea.

Just as quickly as the man came, he had left. I was still in shock, but I could not wait to tell my soldiers. I called over two of my servants and one of my most devout soldiers. Not only was he loyal to me, but he had also seen me praying and begun to have interest in God too. I told them of the messenger, and I know it might have crossed their mind that I was crazy. I was asking them to go into another village and find a man whom they did not know staying as a visitor in another man's house. Not only did they not know Simon the tanner, they also did not know where his house was. My men though were loyal to me, they trusted me. If I said I had a vision from the Lord, and I trusted in that message, they would trust in it too. So, they set off to find the Simon the man they called Peter.

Joppa was only about twenty miles from Caesarea, but travel in my day wasn't as easy as yours is today. I sent my men off on donkeys, but I knew even still it would be a couple days before they arrived back home. I knew they would make it back, and I knew they would bring back Peter. I knew this Peter must have some great purpose. He had to; he was sent by God to us. While the men were away, I sent for my family and close friends to come and join me at my house, so they too could witness this great orchestration of God's work.

When my men returned, with them was Peter, I fell at his feet. I knew it would happen, I knew he would return with my men, but to see it actually happening, I was speechless. The only word I could utter was wow. Wow! Peter reminded me he was just a man and not to worship him. It was just that he had embodied the very works of God. Peter explained that as a Jew in a gentile's house he felt uncomfortable, as it was against the law. However, he spoke of his dream that he had prior to my men arriving. God had shown him that he should not call anyone impure or unclean. That it is what comes out of us that makes us unclean. Upon seeing the gentiles that were willing and seeking God, he realized that God does not show favoritism to any nation, He accepts everyone from every nation that fears

Him and does what is right according to Him. Peter was blessed by us that day, and we were blessed by him.

I have thought of that memory many times. Every time I am in awe. If either of us had not been obedient to the Lord, we both would have missed out on the blessing that God had in store for us. While Peter was there, he spoke of the good news that he had been sent to the people of Israel. He spoke about the rumors we had heard about John the Baptist, and God anointing Jesus of Nazareth with the Holy Spirit, as well as all the miracles and healing Jesus had done. Peter spoke about everything he and the disciples witnessed during Jesus's life. They spoke about how they had murdered Him, but that God had raised Jesus from the tomb after three days and how it had been empty. He spoke about the prophets, about everyone being forgiven of their sins after His death by believing in God and in Jesus. Peter's words were so impactful, all of us that heard them believed and we received the final part to the trilogy of God. The Holy Spirit came over all of us.

Remember how I said that Peter was blessed by my dream just as I was blessed by his, and how our obedience made way for that blessing? Well, because of our obedience to each of our messages from God, Peter brought Jewish men with him, and I gathered my family and friends, and they too were blessed. The Jewish men who witnessed the Holy Spirit being poured out on us were amazed and fully confirmed what Peter had already spoken of: that God does not show favoritism to any nation. As for my family and friends, their lives were never the same. They had been changed forever with the help of the Holy Spirit.

After a while I returned home to Rome after my assignment was over. I was able to return and tell of my interactions with Peter, but most importantly I was able to tell of the love of God, and what Jesus had done for me. It was hard for people to understand as the words I was speaking were coming from a Roman leader. They had such respect for me as a Roman centurion that though they could not understand, they listened because of the respect they had for me. Not all who I told found the same love I had, but some did. And those who did not, I can only assume that a seed was planted, and I'll keep praying that someone comes along and waters that seed. I know that God will place someone at just the right time, in just the right manner to harvest those seeds just as He did with me. It is my greatest hope that every seed I plant will be harvested, but the truth is, it is not the harvest that I am to worry about. I am only to focus on telling others about him. Otherwise, I might get distracted and become ineffective at spreading the gospel.

Acts10:1-Acts 11:18.

Jailer

In my younger days, I was a strong soldier. I could stand tall with my wide shoulders squared off and my head held high. I was proud of my country, proud of my work. I led men through battle and saw my fair share of victories. My men respected me, and we worked well as a unit. That is until it all changed.

When I look back on that night that changed everything, I cannot comprehend how the series of events unfolded or how everything worked out the way it did. There were no battles going on, our country was enjoying a time of peace. The king had asked me and my men to deliver a message to an ally, asking to join us in building a base to secure out southern border. We set off on the journey with no real concern for safety. My men and I were riding along on the backs of our donkeys, when the next thing I knew I was waking up with my men standing over me. It turns out that a snake was along the path. As I went along the path, leading my men, my donkey scared the snake and he wretched back and struck my donkey, biting his leg. This in turn startled my donkey throwing me to the ground where I landed on a rock. It knocked me out. I awoke, in excruciating pain, to my men putting ropes on me so that they could secure me to the donkey of my most loyal soldier. They knew they needed to take me back to our village. I looked around for my donkey, I saw him up ahead lying on the ground. My men told me the snake had been poisonous and it had not taken long for the poison to kill him.

My men secured me to another donkey, and we began the long ride back to the village. It took the entire rest of the day to ride back. With every shift of the donkey I felt stabbing pains in my abdomen and my shoulders. I did not know what all had happened to me, but I knew I had many broken bones. The look in the other soldiers' eyes told me I looked as awful as I felt. I saw pity in their eyes, but more than pity I saw fear.

Upon returning to the village, the doctor looked me over and set my broken shoulder back in place. He wrapped my abdomen, which he was confident held many broken ribs. I also broke my knee when I landed on it. He said I was lucky I landed on my leg first, though bending it backwards had broken my knee, he said that break had saved me from breaking my back and neck. He said that slowed the impact and would have likely resulted in instant death. At that moment though, sitting at the home of the doctor, I would have welcomed instant death. It had to be better than the level of pain I was in. What the doctor told me after assessing my injuries though, hurt worse and hurt longer than any of my broken bones. The doctor said, "With all these injuries you'll be lucky if you survive; but even if you do, your days of being a soldier are over. Your body will never move as quickly or easily as it ever did before." I was crushed. Being a soldier was how I made my living, but more than that, being a soldier was how I supported my country. Being a soldier was my source of pride. Being a soldier was who I was. What I learned many years later was that sometimes we must be broken, before we can be fixed.

After my body began to heal itself, it was never exactly right. I cricked and cracked in ways I had never heard before. It locked in ways it wasn't supposed to and gave out in inconvenient moments that often left me on the ground. The doctor's words ran true, my career as a soldier was over. I was still a young man though, with a family to feed. I could not let this accident be the death of my family. So, as I watched my village to see where I could be of use, and how I could make money, I realized our village needed a way to secure the criminals. Our population was growing, and it was no longer easy for our soldiers to take the prisoners to the next village.

My men came to visit me whenever they could. I may have been injured, but we were still good friends. After talking it over with them and my commanding officer, it was decided that a jail would be built on my property and my new assignment was to be the jailer. My job as the jailer was to make sure that no prisoner ever escaped. Over time we had built a wall around our original jail cell, which was built into a cave, then a wall around that jail cell, and finally a wall around my property. That inner jail cell had stocks that kept prisoners' feet and hands secure. It had little light and was reserved for the worst of the worst criminals. For the most devious of criminals that were at risk of escaping. Because the inner cell was built into a cave, it also had the advantage of echoing throughout the prison so prisoners grouped in the cell could not plot, because it would be spoiled by anyone wanting to listen in.

As months turned into years, we saw many prisoners come and go. Some petty crimes, others much more serious. In all my years though, my family never had one prisoner escape. Just as I had taken pride in being a soldier, so did I on being a jailer. I was good at it. My boys would be good at it too. The success of our jail was our livelihood. I remember the night I thought it had all come to an end. The night I thought my life, and the life of my family was over. The night I almost died. Truth is, as I say that, I can also say, it was the night I died, and He lived.

A man by the name of Paul and a man by the name of Silas were brought to me. I was commanded to guard them carefully. I knew not what their crime had been, but I did know their reputation. I knew they had been traveling and causing an uproar wherever they went. Because they were not from this village, I knew if they got loose, they would run, and I would pay with my life for failing. So, I took both men, and I locked them in stocks in the inner cell. After I secured their stocks, I walked away leaving them in the cave with little light. After night had fallen, I could hear them praising the very king they had been accused of speaking about in the market. I could not believe it. How could they praise this king they talked about, this king that had caused them to be locked up in the first place? Yet they did, and they kept doing so. Because they were in the inner cell every other prisoner could hear them. They all listened to them praise this king. After listening myself for a little while, I went back to my quarters shaking my head at how crazy these men were.

It was sometime after I had fallen asleep that I was violently shaken awake. At first, I did not know what had happened. Then I realized we were in the midst of a large earthquake. I immediately ran to the prison cells on the other side of my property and stopped dead in my tracks when I saw what had happened. Panicked to took off to the inner cells and there stood the two men shackle free. The earthquake had opened every gate and broken every shackle. I drew the sword off my side and was prepared to kill myself. Far better it for my family that I do it, than to have the Philippian army do it once they realized I had failed at my mission. As I was about to drag the sword across my throat though, Paul shouted that all the prisoners were accounted for, none had escaped. He said, "Do not harm yourself". I thought to myself, why does he care? Why did he care if I killed myself? If I did then he could escape. Why hadn't he escaped, why hadn't any of the men escaped? How could very shackle and every gate possibly have broken and opened? All these thoughts ran through my head, but I had no answers. I was so confused. I called for my sons to light all the lights and I fell at the feet of Paul and Silas. Nothing made sense, but these two knew. It made sense to them, and they knew the answers. I asked them, "Sirs, what must I do to be saved?" And what they said was so simple, they said, "Believe in the Lord Jesus and you will be saved". Oh, I believed! How could I not believe? I had known they were different when they praised their King, despite being jailed. I knew something was captivating about their praises when none of the imprisoned ran despite being free. I knew something was different when they protected me from murdering myself. Paul and Silas spoke the word of God to me and all who were at my house that day, family servants and prisoners, we all believed.

Paul and Silas, prior to coming to my prison, had been flogged. Because of that they had many wounds. I took them to my living quarters and cleaned all their wounds. Immediately everyone in my house was baptized and we had a meal together. I was filled with such joy and peace. I did not know what would become of Paul and Silas, or what would become of me and my family, but I knew they would not be going back to the inner cell, not under my watch.

It did not take long to learn what would happen to them. The magistrate sent officers to let us know that Paul and Silas could leave. I was so relieved to know their suffering was coming to an end. But then Paul said no, that telling them to leave without an announcement or public forum would not be acceptable. They could not simply flog Roman citizens in the town center, falsely imprison them and then brush off the issue as if it did not happen. My heart began to race. If they were Roman citizens and everything that had happened to them had been illegal. While I was just following orders, I too had been a part of something illegal. It was then that I realized that Paul was not standing up for himself, but he was actually standing up for every believer, which now included me and my family. Paul and Silas had been flogged, not because of the accusations that had been brought against them, but because they were sharing the love of Jesus and what His life came to represent. They were telling people about a power higher than the Roman king in charge and they did not like that. He was taking power away from evil beings and they would not stand for it.

I wept with sorrow for the role I played. In this ugly power-hungry lust, I had caused harm to these men, who despite all of that, gave me their time to save my life. Paul had seen my sorrow. He told me he recognized it in himself. He told me his story, about how God forgives and changes us. I was so thankful that God had brought Paul and Silas into my life. Even though there was sorrow, it was worth it.

I did not know what my life would hold after Paul and Silas left, but I knew it would be different. I knew I would have to stand against that power hungry culture, and it likely meant I would pay for it with my life. But I was ready, I was willing. I had to be because Jesus already had been for me.

Acts 16:16-40

Nicodemus

My name is Nicodemus, I was a teacher of the law, a man very well-versed in scripture. I am also a man who is ashamed to be linked together with a group called the Pharisees. I am not ashamed of being a Pharisee, but ashamed of how they are known to have treated a man named Jesus. A man, I am sure was much more than a man. This is the story I tell about my encounter with Jesus, and how He changed me from a teacher of a law, to a man born again of the Spirit.

This man, Jesus, a man from Galilee, came into our land, and He began teaching. The Pharisees, as teachers of the law we were well-versed in scripture. We had learned to interpret that scripture as it pertained to our law. What Jesus was teaching did not agree with what we taught from the law. He healed as well as taught on the Sabbath. He kept company with the lowest of lows. People began to see these miracles of healing and hear His words. They were captivated by it. They began to follow Him everywhere, which meant they began to not follow us-teachers of the law. We were losing control, we were losing our power. My fellow teachers of the law began to hate this man from Galilee named Jesus. His teachings threatened our very way of life. Whenever we crossed paths there were always heated arguments and accusations thrown about. Even so, there was something about Him that I could not place my finger on. How could He do these miracles without being from God? I did not share these nagging questions deep in my soul with any of my fellow teachers. They would have raked me over the coals, much like they did Jesus. I knew I wanted to know more, I needed to know more.

Under the cloak of darkness, I met up with Jesus, and I took the opportunity to ask Him questions. The questions my forever-student heart wanted to know. I wanted to learn, but I could not dare ask Him when others were around. Jesus spoke of being born again, born of spirit instead of flesh. It did not make sense, so I asked Him how this could be, and he said, "I have spoken of earthly things, and you did not believe. How then will you believe if I speak of heavenly things?" He was absolutely right. I knew that if I wanted to know more, if I wanted to be taught, I would have to change. I would have to believe what He spoke of when He taught here on Earth. Then I could gain knowledge on this spirit and how to become born again. It was an odd theory, but I left that night a changed man. I left believing that not only was this man a teacher, but He was also sent by God, He was the Messiah.

From that point on, I began to listen to what people said He was teaching them. I listened during every interaction He had with the Pharisees. The interactions began to escalate. The Pharisees had come to the conclusion that Jesus had to be executed. The threat needed to be removed. I tried convincing my fellow Pharisees that our law does not condemn a man without first hearing him out. But they were convinced that a man from such a small insignificant town such as Galilee was incapable of producing a prophet. I thought to myself, you haven't even asked Him where He is from. But what could I do? They were dead set on the plan. They had long since given up listening to sound logic. They were right and there was no possibility they could be wrong. They had determined His fate. Had they though?

I had been listening to what He said, what others said He said. Jesus had been known to predict His death and subsequent resurrection. That night when I snuck out to meet him, He had said, "Just as Moses lifted up the snake in the wilderness, so the Son of Man must be lifted up". People said He talked about how the Son of Man must be lifted up. I began to realize that Jesus knew He had to die, that He was actually working towards that, so that He could be lifted up. It left me to wonder, were the Pharisees seeking out Jesus to kill Him actually part of the plan? Were they unknowingly participants in God's master plan to save the people? Was Jesus the ultimate sacrifice? I had so many unanswered questions, but what I no longer had was a belief so locked in legalism that I missed the Messiah right there in front of me.

Jesus was ultimately crucified, as an innocent man. The Pharisees felt victorious. It was at that moment with my heart broken and religion shattered that I walked away from being a Pharisee. I turned my back on my band of brothers. I joined others to give Jesus the proper burial He deserved. I brought the spices, and we wrapped Him in the linen and spices. That day as a broken man, I somehow felt whole. I was now a follower of Jesus, the Son of Man, the Messiah. He saved my soul.

In these last words I want to leave you with this thought. I can tell you about Jesus. I can tell you about His life, I can tell you about my experiences, but I cannot build a relationship with Jesus for you. Only you can do that. Only you can seek Him for yourself. Only you can be obedient to the call He has on your life. Only you can tell your story.

John 3:1-15
John 7:32-52
John 19:38-42

Vulnerability

I did not write these fictionalized testimonies from real life biblical characters for entertainment purposes. Though I did enjoy writing them, and I do hope you enjoyed reading them just as much. The Holy Spirit has given me this intense message on my heart to share with other believers. To encourage them and to ignite in them a call to action. Every single believer reading this book, actually let me rephrase that, every single believer, not just the ones reading this book, have not just one, but many testimonies to share. You have your initial story on how Jesus found you, often times lost, broken and alone. Some of the stories might be how He found you as a little child, some as an old man. Either way, everyone has that story of how they first came to know Jesus. That is often referred to as your testimony, but might I suggest a change of thinking is in order!

According to Webster dictionary testimony is defined as a statement testifying to benefits received. So, we only receive benefits from our Lord, Jesus Christ one time and that's it? No, absolutely not. Every answered prayer, every rescued situation, every lesson taught…are those not benefits? Of course! So, in turn those benefits are your testimonies.

So, we have established that every believer has testimonies to share. Doing so though requires vulnerability. When telling someone about how God saved you, changed you, taught you or answered your prayers, it requires the before. How you once were, and then how you now are. The before and the after. However, for many people, that before has shame attached to it. We do not want to tell the before so, consequently we do not tell the after. We do not give God the glory because we do not want to give ourselves the shame.

Social media has, in my opinion, really ramped up this perfect life persona that people take on. Before social media, there was still the "keeping up with the Beavers", but that ended when the front door closed. You could escape the need to be perfect. However, now with social media at everyone's fingertips, our every intimate moment is broadcast for the world to see. Well, every intimate moment we choose to share. Now you see the great flowers the husband bought his wife for no reason at all, you see the perfectly decorated wall or room, you see the smiling faces and everyone's picture-perfect life. What we do not hear is the harsh tone demanding that smiling face, the other side of the room where everything was shoved out of the way for the perfectly decorated room picture. We do not hear the argument that brought on the guilt that prompted the purchase of the "no reason at all" flowers. A picture might be worth a thousand words, but it still does not tell the whole story, or sometimes even the truth. Perception, lighting, angles, they can all be deceiving. Most of us know this, yet we still fall victim to our mental comparisons. We compare our reality to someone else's display of perfect reality.

So, with the perfect life being displayed, being vulnerable is understandably terrifying. Let me remind you though, that God is NOT the author of fear, Satan is. You see, vulnerability is an incredibly powerful tool in God's tool belt. Being real and showing how you once were and how He has changed you, both with your actions and your words, is a way to encourage others, believers and unbelievers alike. Contrary to what Satan would like you to believe, you are not alone in your struggle. There are people out there just like you, struggling the same way you once did. When you are willing to be vulnerable and tell them how God turned things around for you, it gives them hope. Just as there are people out there struggling just like you once did, there are people out there who once struggled just like you are right at this moment. Even more, there are people struggling the same way you are at this same exact moment in time. The words might be a little different, the source of the problem might be a little different, but the struggle is the same, I guarantee it. You know how I know? Because Satan does not have any new tricks up his sleeves. He does not need any new tricks because the old ones still work. He does not want you to be vulnerable because it exposes the lie in one of his biggest schemes, which is to convince you that you are alone, that nobody else could ever understand your struggle. It is a bunch of hooey though. I am willing to bet that if we started using social media to showcase the schemes of Satan in our lives and glorifying God, we'd see just how basic his schemes are. But that would call for us to put ourselves willingly into a place of vulnerability.

Now do not get me wrong, I am not suggesting that we post complaining about everything happening to us. People would stop reading our posts. I am also not suggesting that everything bad that happens is from Satan. No matter how well we take care of our cars, there is going to come a time when something goes out on it, that's reality. But sometimes Satan sneaks in and torments you to distract you. For example, as I write this, I am two weeks out from doing my first speaking event. To say that I am nervous would be an understatement. I know that the message given to me is from the Holy Spirit, but I just do not want to screw it up. If you read my first book, you will know that I always struggle with not living up to what I am supposed to do. Anyway, two weeks ago my shower broke. I have not been able to shower at home. I tried fixing it myself but could not. I did not want people to know that my shower broke. I did not want them to know that I was taking bird baths and washing my hair in the kitchen sink. I was completely embarrassed, I was ashamed. At first, I let the anxiety take over. About a week into it, I realized this was a first world problem. Some people do not have running water at all, and here I am embarrassed that I have a shower that is not working. I had taken my eyes off Jesus and had them on other people and how they would perceive things. After I got my eyes back on Jesus, I realized that Satan was trying to distract me, to steal, kill and destroy my peace, my focus and ultimately, he wants me to quit and not share the message God had laid on my heart. Once I focused back on what God called me to do and remained in prayer with Jesus, a peace grew in me. I was no longer distracted by the shower issue. I had peace about the shower being fixed, and He calmed my nerves about my speaking engagement.

I image that this story, this scheme of Satan, rings familiar with someone reading it. It might not be your shower that broke, but something came up in your life to distract you from your purpose. Seeing the schemes are from Satan, requires us to look past the surface level issues going on in our life and see what the results of the situation are. This will be a good indicator if Satan is involved and if he is scheming in our lives.

Do you see what I just did there? I allowed myself to be vulnerable. I told of the before, the part that brought me shame. That part was followed up with how it was resolved and gave God the glory. That was a testimony. That was me testifying to a benefit I received from God. So, you see, a testimony does not have to be given at a church service in front of everyone, it doesn't even need to be in a book. A social media post can be a testimony. Talking with a friend and encouraging them with how God has helped you, that is sharing your testimony. Exposing yourself to friends while you are still going through it and have not yet seen the benefit is also a testimony. It says I have not yet come through the other side, but I am trusting in my Lord to help me through.

Being vulnerable allows us to plow through the walls that we allow Satan to build up around us and it breaks the chains Satan has tried to bound us with. These chains are an attempt to make us ineffective for God, ineffective in what it is God has called us to do. Not only that, but it also heavily damages the walls he has built around others too. That is why time and time again in scripture we see Jesus call people to be vulnerable and share their story. Vulnerability is a powerful tool for God, and it is a powerful weapon against Satan. In this next chapter we will explore how it is not just a good idea, but it is a command.

Call to Action

"Go home to your own people and tell them how much the Lord has done for you, and how he has had mercy on you." Mark 5:19-NIV

These words were spoken by Jesus. He had just restored a man who was so tormented by demons that he could not be subdued by anyone or anything. No chains would secure him, though they had tried many of times. He constantly, without regard to night or day, would cry out. He cut himself with stones. With open sores and incessant hollering, unable to be secured, he was no longer even regarded as a citizen. He was possessed with not one, but a legion of demons. Jesus though, saw him for who he truly was, and cast out the demons from this man into a herd of pigs. After the demons were cast out the man was dressed and in his right mind. Jesus restored him by removing his demons. The man begged to go with Jesus, but Jesus told him to go home to his own people. I am sure this man wanted to be with the only person who saw him as a human being, and that going back home to the people who had abandoned him was not what his heart wanted. I think seeing this man restored to his own mind in and of itself would have been a great testimony, but Jesus does not stop at go home to your own people. He says, "and tell them how much the Lord has done for you, and how he has had mercy on you". You see, if they had seen his restoration that would have been amazing, and they would have believed in the miracles of God. However, if the man were to go home and tell of how Jesus had seen him as a human being, despite his ghastly appearances and awful behavior, if he were to tell of the gentleness Jesus had with him, that would speak to a level far beyond the healing miracle they could see with their own eyes. When he would have spoken about the mercy, he would be teaching them how to have compassion, how to love on the level that Jesus did.

**"Many of the Samaritans from that town believed in him because of the woman's testimony, 'He told me everything I ever did."
John 4:39 NIV**

We met the woman at the well earlier in the book, we heard what her testimony may have sounded like. We saw how her behavior had brought her to a point of such shame. Then she has an interaction with Jesus that shakes her world. She goes back into town and tells the people about it. This interaction was evidently so powerful that her shame was less important than telling the people. Because of that, we see that many people believed in Jesus as a result of her testimony. She brings many people back who want to meet Jesus for themselves, and it says in vs 42, "They said to the woman, 'We no longer believe just because of what you said; now we have heard for ourselves, and we know that this man really is the Savior of the world'." (John 4:42 NIV). You see, God can use just your words to open people's hearts. When your words become their reality, and they see and witness God for themselves, it solidifies that belief.

"Therefore, go and make disciples of all nations, baptizing them in the name of the Father and the Son and of the Holy Spirit, and teaching them to obey everything that I have commanded you. And surely, I am with you always, to the very end of the age." Matthew 28:19-20 NIV

Many of us know this to be the great commission. You might think well this is not telling us to go and testify to people, but it is. If you walked up to someone on the street and said I am going to baptize you in the name of the Father and the Son and of the Holy Spirit, I do not think they would take kindly to that. If they do, and they are willing to be baptized, will they even know what that means?

In order to accept help, you have to first be willing to accept that you need help. Take for instance a toddler trying to open something. You ask them if they need some help, and they respond back, "Me do it!" This might even go on for a while, but if you were to yank it out of their hands and open it, I am guessing a full-on tantrum would follow. Not to mention, children learn by example and yanking something out of their hands, well that is not a good lesson to be taught. It is not until the toddler brings you the object to be opened, the point in which they are willingly accepting that they need help, that they are willing to receive said help. As unbelievers we were no different. Until we were willing to admit that we were sinners in need of a savior, we were not interested in what believers are saying. Offering a savior to someone who does not think they sin may or may not result in a full-blown tantrum, but it definitely will not result in a willing heart.

If they are unwilling to admit that they are in need of savior, they most likely are not welcome to the idea of listening to you talk about the gospel. So, if we have a group of people who refuse to admit they need help, who refuse to listen to scripture, but we are to go and make disciples of all nations, what are we to do, quit? Or keep forcing the scripture? I do not think either of these options are valuable or correct.

We know that there are people in this world, past, current, and future that have hardened hearts and will never be willing to accept Jesus Christ as their savior. We see examples in scripture of people whose hearts were hardened, such as the Pharaoh during Moses' time in Exodus. His heart was hardened. We can see it in the future generation that is still yet to come in Revelations when Jesus is revealed in the sky, and they still refuse to believe. And if people are the same, past and future, then sadly there are people living among us whose hearts are hardened as well, and they will never believe in

Jesus. But we know not who they are. So, if hardened hearts are out there…and we do not know who is hardened or not…and we are called to go and make disciples of all nations…then I think we must use all the tools in our tool belts.

We see Jesus meets the tax collectors, prostitutes, and sinners right where they were. If we are called to live like Jesus did, which we are, then we too are called to meet people right where they are. That means adjusting our approach to each person. When we tell of Jesus, if a person is unwilling to admit they need a savior, and unwilling to listen to scripture, maybe perhaps they are willing to hear your story. Praying, asking for guidance on how to share your story, listening, and discerning how to meet people is incredibly important. Because zeal without wisdom can be just as dangerous and wisdom without zeal.

When we share our story though, as I have stated before, it has two parts, the before Jesus, and the after. When we tell how life was before we speak of his mercy, when we speak of how Jesus entered our life, and when we speak of the change, we are actually sharing the gospel of Jesus Christ, even if it is in disguise. Seeing themselves in someone else sometimes is the catalyst God will use, so that they might realize they too are in need of a savior, and consequently be open to hearing the scripture.

God can use scripture, prayer, testimonies, tragic events, anything and everything to change the course of people's lives. He knows their hearts, He knows what they need in order to believe, and He is the great orchestrator. All we have to do is listen to His prompting, be obedient and use the tools He has given us.

"You will be his witness to all people of what you have seen and heard. And now what are you waiting for? Get up, be baptized and wash

your sins away, calling on his name." Acts 22:15-16 NIV

This scripture says you will bear witness to what you have seen and heard. This is not just taking the gospel and teaching from scripture; this is testifying to the works of God that you have seen and heard. Some of these are from scripture, some of which are not. Please do not take this to mean that I want to elevate personal experience over scripture, which is not the case. There is a time and a place where scripture is the preferred method that God will use to open someone's heart. I love scripture, I love studying scripture and I am not trying to diminish its purpose. Sometimes though, the chosen instrument of God is sharing your experiences. That initial opening of the heart allows for the love of God to grow and with that, their desire to learn scripture. God determines which method He is prompting us to, He knows what will and will not penetrate a heart. That is why I spoke earlier of discernment and prayer to help determine how we are to move forward. Equal amounts of zeal and wisdom, along with equal amounts truth and grace.

In these scripture examples that call us to action, we see commands. Not in the "Thou Shall Not..." commands, but in use of action words that do not leave any wiggle room. We see GO, a command. It does not say you might want to go, or it is probably a good idea if you go, it says GO. It is followed by specifically what to do when you go. It says tell what the Lord has done for you and of his grace. It is not vague for a reason, there is no question left in the man's mind what he is called to do. Again, we see Go and specific instructions in the Great Commission scripture.

Finally in that last scripture I listed, it says you WILL BE. It does not say might be, or should be, it says you WILL BE. And then as if we did not already know how well God knows us, He calls us out in our tendency to drag our feet. He says what are you waiting for? Get up (another command). So, I pose this question to you, "What are you waiting for"? God did not leave us any wiggle room in His commands. To make excuses, however valid we feel they are, we are still being disobedient. God does not have excuses for us when we come to Him. Why then should we, when He calls on us?

Moving Past Our Excuses

In this book I have talked about the different kinds of ways to share our testimony, publicly, with social media and privately. Scripture tells us in 1 Peter 3:15 "But in your hearts revere Christ as Lord. Always be prepared to give an answer to everyone who asks you to give the reason for the hope that you have. But do this with gentleness and respect." We are called to ALWAYS be prepared. That means no matter when, where, or how someone asks us, we need to be prepared to always be able to answer that question of why Jesus. If you feel a nudging to share your testimony, your praise, the benefit you have received, there is only one thing I can guarantee you: it ain't Satan. Satan does not want you to give the Glory to God, he does not want you to expose the lie that you're alone, he doesn't want you to encourage other people. As with everything there are two extremes. That nudging could be pride, but it ain't pride either if you're dreading doing it.

In this chapter I would like to help you (and in turn myself) conquer some common schemes of Satan that prevents us from stepping out. I will briefly outline some of them. Remember, the details will be different for each person, but once we look past the surface, we will see these schemes take form.

NOBODY THINKS, ACTS, OR FEELS THE WAY I DO

The first excuse is one we have talked about a lot, and I do not know how to let you know any more than I already have. YOU ARE NOT ALONE. This is one that I struggle with all the time. I do not know anyone in a situation like mine, and so I constantly feel like I have no one to talk to, no one who would understand. It is a lie, they might not fully understand the details of your situation, but they want to be there for you, for me. While they might not understand the details of your struggles, I guarantee they understand the feelings that result from it. I do not want to sit here and type this out and pretend this is not a daily struggle for me, just because I know the answer, does not make it any easier. Scripture says we are not ignorant of the schemes of Satan, it does not say we never fall for or struggle with them despite knowing them.

I'M TOO AFRAID

The next excuse is fear, this is multifaceted, and by that, I mean fear comes from all sorts of different directions and I cannot possibly attack all the angles. But I can attack the main source. Scripture tells us that God is not the author of fear, Satan is. God will not prompt you to be immobilized. Satan is the only one who wants you to stop. One way to counter fear is accountability. If you feel called to do something, tell someone you trust so they can hold you accountable. It is super easy to let fear conquer you and quit when nobody is counting on you to follow through. Finally, the last part is a pride check. Is your fear more important than someone else's salvation? I know this might hurt to hear, but when we are too afraid to share our testimony, we could be robbing someone else of the hope that they need that will break open their heart. In turn we are robbing ourselves of seeing that joy and of hearing how our words were an encouragement. We are robbing both parties of a blessing.

I'M NOT SMART ENOUGH

The third excuse we tend to use is, I do not know what to say. I am not prepared. The next chapter will help conquer this excuse. It is a worksheet that I hope can help you to prepare your testimony. My third book will be called "The Story You Tell". It is my hope that if this book has inspired you to tell your story, that you will share it with me. "The Story You Tell", will be a compilation of testimonies from everyday people. In 1 Peter

3:16 scripture says "But in your hearts revere Christ as Lord. Always be prepared to give an answer to everyone who asks you to give the reason for the hope that you have. But do this with gentleness and respect". It says be prepared, that is a command. You do not magically become prepared. It takes some thought and effort. We have to work to become prepared. Some will not need the worksheet; I imagine, for some, if you take some time and sit down at a computer it will pour out of you. However, I also know that I have been called to include this worksheet, so I know that for some it will not just pore out. My hope is that you do not just read this book and put it down without a renewed or increased desire to share your testimonies. We just have to put the excuses behind us and get prepared.

BUT I'M NOT A.....

The fourth excuse right now is one I struggle with hard core. "I'm not a public speaker, I do not like being in the limelight, I much prefer the behind-the-scenes task." God calls us to grow, to stretch beyond our grasp of possibilities. If we are obedient, He will take us far beyond our own comprehensions. If you had told me three years ago that I would write a book, get a publishing contract and be speaking in public, I would have said you have the wrong girl. Even today, I cannot comprehend that I am coming to a close on my second book. In a week and a half, I will be doing my first public speaking event. I constantly think to myself, but I'm not.... However, God does not call the qualified, He qualifies the called. God has already laid on my heart what my mission is, and God will give me the opportunities to grow in whatever capacity He knows that I need. Not what I think I need or do not need. I have made up my mind that I will not allow myself to give excuses to not to do what He has called me to. He knows far better than I do what I am capable of. I do not want to stand in the way of His progress. I will not let my fear or excuses be elevated above God and above what He has called me to do.

Just so Satan cannot take my words and twist them to mean something different to the reader, I would like to clarify. I am not saying nobody should be afraid of doing the Lord's work. I am saying that nobody should let fear keep them from doing the Lord's work. In Ezra chapter 3 verse 3 says "Despite their fear of the peoples around them, they built the altar on its foundation and sacrificed burnt offerings on it to the Lord, both morning and evening sacrifices." We are going to have fear, sometimes justified, sometimes not. Despite that, we cannot let that fear dictate what we do and do not do. That is what bondage is, but Jesus came to set us free. We have to fight past the fear and do what the Lord is calling us to. We have to be obedient despite our fears.

Above I have listed some common excuses and fears that Satan has used on me. It is not an exclusive list of the way Satan works by any means. If none of these excuses pertain to you, I challenge you to seek in prayer what it is that is holding you back and ask God to help you move past whatever that is. I guarantee that if the fear is keeping you for doing what the Lord has called you to, it is Satan sparked and flesh fulfilled. This kind of fear requires spiritual warfare to battle, so let us suit up in the full armor of Christ because He has called ALL of us to a life living His purpose and his call on our life.

Worksheet & Prayer Guide

"Do not be anxious about anything, but in every situation, by prayer and petition, with thanksgiving, present your requests to God." Philippians 4:6

The following worksheet will be a guide to anyone who is struggling to tell their story. My first recommendation is to pray, ask God to give you the words to tell your story. To help you find, refine, or reignite the calling on your life. Then, sit down and put pen to paper or fingers to the keyboard and be surprised at how the words begin to flow. However, if the words still do not flow, use the following worksheet to get you thinking and remembering. Either way, use this time to do what Philippians 4:6 says. Come with your prayers, your petitions, always with your praise for his glory.

1. **Where did you first hear about God or Jesus? What was your attitude towards what you heard? How did the person telling you react? If negatively, did that impact you?**

Some came to hear about Jesus, and what he did for them at a young age. Some grew up in the church. This question is not about when you first believed, but instead the first interaction with the name of Jesus. This could be through a church service, through someone yelling on the street corner, or even through a co-worker.

2.   When was the moment you decided to give Jesus a try? Was it right away or did it take some time before you prayed the sinner's prayer?

Some people have a big aha moment where everything changes in an instant. For others perhaps it was a bottom of the barrel moment where they could not continue that direction in life, and they beg for help. Perhaps it is a series of seemingly coincidental events that you could no longer ignore. Whatever the moment or time looked like, all our moments have one thing in common. We prayed, even if we did not realize it was a prayer, and we said Lord, I'm sorry, please help me.

3.   How did the minutes, hours, days, weeks and first couple of months look like after you first prayed the sinner's prayer? How did your friends and family act? What impact did their reaction have on you?

Oftentimes, when we first come to Jesus, we want to tell the whole world about this man named Jesus that changed our life. Sometimes, that zeal and fire we have for Jesus is squelched by the reaction from friends and family. Sometimes we are afraid to lose the friends or family we had. Satan helps us get distracted by those reactions and the fear sets in and soon we're sharing less and less about Jesus.

4.   As the months turn into years since praying the sinner's prayer, we begin to fall into a routine of life as a Christian. We begin to fall prey to the distractions of the daily grind of life. Where has the daily grind of life brought you? Are you satisfied with where you are in your walk?

If you are not satisfied, make it a part of your prayer. Lord, thank you for saving me from myself, from the direction in life I was headed. I am so incredibly thankful for your grace and mercy in my life, but I also want to go deeper with you, Lord. I want to learn more of your word, I want to learn how to walk more like you, Jesus. I want to rid more and more of myself so there is more and more room for you, Jesus. Show me how I can grow, break me so you can build me stronger. When we say this prayer, we have to be prepared that the refining process comes with fire. Where there is fire, we will be burned, but He's making us better, not because He wants to hurt us, but because He wants more for us.

5.   How have you seen God work in the lives of other people? Perhaps it was strength given to someone on incomprehensible levels. Maybe it was a healing of body or mind. Maybe it was a miracle of an answered prayer.

As we grow in our faith, we take on more difficult roles in the life of other believers. We see things, hear things, and understand things on a different level. Not a better level, just a different level. Thus far the questions have been about your first testimony. About how you once were, the moment you found Jesus and how life is different now. However, testimony is not limited to the first time Jesus changed you. He is continuously changing us, and sometimes the change is not what happened in our own lives, but how we've seen God work in the lives of others. These moments impacted both parties, and that is a story to tell as well.

6. Finally the last question is not one to be answered by you, but more a question to ask God. Lord, use me. Show me how I can live out my life living the purpose you have called me to. Show me what I need to do, what I need to work on, where I need to go. Show me the opportunities to share my testimony. Show me the opportunities to share your story Lord.

Other titles from Higher Ground Books & Media:

Bits & Pieces by Rebecca Whited

Finding Purpose in the Pain by Brenda W. McIntire

God's Whispers by Christine Nekas-Thoma

Raven Transcending Fear by Terri Kozlowski

The Power of Knowing by Jean Walters

Forgiven and Not Forgotten by Terra Kern

Through the Sliver of a Frosted Window by Robin Melet

Breaking the Cycle by Willie Deeanjlo White

Healing in God's Power by Yvonne Green

The Frost of Lost Words by Stephen Shepherd

The Real Prison Diaries by Judy Frisby

The Words of My Father by Mark Nemetz

The Bottom of This by Tramaine Hannah

Add these titles to your collection today!

http://www.highergroundbooksandmedia.com

HIGHER GROUND BOOKS & MEDIA IS

AN INDEPENDENT PUBLISHER

Do you have a story to tell?

Higher Ground Books & Media is an independent Christian-based publisher specializing in stories of triumph! Our purpose is to empower, inspire, and educate through the sharing of personal experiences. We are always looking for great, new stories to add to our collection. If you're looking for a publisher, get in touch with us today!

Please be sure to visit our website for our submission guidelines.

http://www.highergroundbooksandmedia.com/submission-guidelines

---

HGBM SERVICES IS OUR CONSULTING FIRM

AUTHOR SERVICES

HGBM Services offers a variety of writing and coaching services for aspiring authors! We can help with editing, manuscript critiques, self-publishing, and much more! Get in touch today to see how we can help you make your dream of becoming an author a reality!

*****

We also offer social media marketing services for authors, small businesses, and non-profit organizations. Let us help you get the word out about your book, your projects, and your mission. We offer great rates, quality promos, consistent communication, and a personal touch!

http://www.highergroundbooksandmedia.com/editing-writing-services

Need Bulk Copies?

If you would like to order bulk copies of this book or any other title at Higher Ground Books & Media, please contact us at highergroundbooksandmedia@gmail.com.

We offer discounts for purchases of 20 or more copies. Excellent for small groups, book clubs, classrooms, etc.

Get in touch today and get a set of great stories for your students or group members.